The Schizophrenic Table
Poems New and Selected

Chris Clendenin

THE SCHIZOPHRENIC TABLE
POEMS NEW AND SELECTED

iUniverse books may be ordered through booksellers or by contacting:

iUniverse
1663 Liberty Drive
Bloomington, IN 47403
www.iuniverse.com
844-349-9409

Because of the dynamic nature of the Internet, any web addresses or links contained in this book may have changed since publication and may no longer be valid. The views expressed in this work are solely those of the author and do not necessarily reflect the views of the publisher, and the publisher hereby disclaims any responsibility for them.

Any people depicted in stock imagery provided by Getty Images are models, and such images are being used for illustrative purposes only. Certain stock imagery © Getty Images.

ISBN: 978-1-6632-2599-3 (sc)
ISBN: 978-1-6632-2600-6 (e)

Print information available on the last page.

iUniverse rev. date: 07/15/2021

For Wild Jeanne

A table which lent itself to no function,
self-protective, denying itself to service
and communication alike. There was some-
thing stunned about it, something petrified.
Perhaps it suggested a stalled engine.

—Henri Michaux

Contents

Acknowledgments

Skanky Possum ("Do," "Worse than Your Worst").
The Quarterly ("Church of San Solitudo").
College English ("Cheese Storm").
Wascana Review ("Lent").
The American Poetry Review ("Out of Sight, Out of Mind").
Allbook Books Haiku Calendar (Haiku)

The Schizophrenic Table

Incurably hungry
absorbent as an abandoned shaft
it eats its reasons
for being here.
Losing without having had, it hurts.
It is its own encroacher.
When the room is dark
the tabletop diffuses
fear (the knuckles of its
hips engorging it).
This is why
when I give it a bouquet
it accepts it as a well accepts
a wooden spoon.
It grew itself to death
tunneled to bedrock and
stopped.
When it wakes
it will be a well of
living rock.

Cheese Storm

The first flakes fell before Barnaby's opened for breakfast.
Farmers flapped their hats.
Early laundry whitened on the lines.
A housecat lapped her powdered back and bit herself.
Hiding under fenders, dozing on the picnic tables in the shelter house
or watching from the ends of drains, cats had made up their minds.
Woodwork sighed mice by the million.
Children sledded on the hill behind the
Home, tossed balls to the dogs
and barefoot made great men.
Tommy Jacob made a Lincoln.
Noon the drifts began to sweat, the drains
ran whey and the great men
wet with buttermilk fed many happy cats.

Do

Any change at first is an improvement.
Get a job, quit a job, smoke or stop or try a line of coke or start
collecting nests.
Molest a plant.
Stop waking in the middle of the night.
Stop thinking of the same thing all the time.

Stuck in His Ways

He made them himself in a portable forge.
Tonto pumped the bellows
every Saturday night, Kemosabe
having hacksawed all their dollars
into quarters for the crucible.
Tonto had wondered once
out loud, whether *wooden* bullets
might be nice, mahogany maybe
with a glossy finish.
Or flint, he said, he could do flint
in the saddle, flint in his sleep with his feet in the fire
think about it.
Never had the man in the mask even answered.
He just looked at him like he was crazy.

Lent

This morning stood two ponies in the wind, a frozen wind, side by
side, quivering the hide on their rumps against the stinging
song.
Months from now the pastures bleed
impatient pops of color, indicating
all that is buried there.
Or all that has never come to light.
Now the ponies take no comfort in last year's leavings, in the brittle
sprigs of spring.
They stand side by side in the frozen wind and wait for anything.

Worse than Your Worst

If you succeed, having persevered (in study, near misses and errors)
in calling up a demon, you'll need to succeed in sending it back.
It won't want to go.
You'll need to know what to say to its face.
You'll need to know how to concentrate.

At Bottom

Today I clear the books
out of my bathtub.
Not to make room for myself—
I cut the pipes a year ago
to keep them from freezing—
But to clear the souvenirs
away and the worst
of the books
and roust a rat, someone's rat
that made it up the drain
to nest in my receipts.
An endless dig
in a weary pit of news,
the rat having had
the right idea.

Further Notice

They've closed the cathedral
for redecoration,
Mass in the basement,
no kneelers, music, procession, collection,
almost no ventilation;
someone farts,
it's for the duration,
penitential.
This is the crypt.
For the Lord's Prayer
we stand from our folding
chairs and hold
hands in the crypt,
the old vicar's focus so shaky
we say it twice.

Implant

"They're giving me an implant"
the old man said
"a titanium ball."
Standing at the coffee counter
he swung his arm round
and round
to demonstrate his disability
and frowned
"titanium."
"Sorry" I said
"sounds expensive. What
do they do
with the bad ball?"
Sad to say
this saddened him, recalling
all his ball had done.

If I Took an Intelligence Test

and found out
I'm an idiot
I'd make sense to myself.
As my dentist said
to his hygienist
"Look, just look
what he has to work with."
Discipline and fortitude
morning after
morning
making the most of it.
What an idiot.

Devil's Advocate

The devil gets a lawyer.
Appointed by the court
Advocatus Diaboli
to badmouth would-be saints,
skeptical of miracles
alleging normality
lapses of sanctity
secret vices
jokes about the pope.
He can win
as when they took away
Mister Christopher's day.
He can lose
and just like that
cobblers
get an advocate of their own.

Trust Me

I stated my name
and the polygraph
perked up and hissed
that I lied
when I said yes
I am here
and reside nearby
in a small brown house
and have never been a
communist.
Liar
it said
you are not unmarried
and you lie to your wife.
I admitted petty theft
and it rejected
my confession
since I didn't exist
which is why faucets
ignore me
and I too easily
think of nothing
and remember nothing
of myself.

How Light Falls on the Long Haul

Quality Beef on the Move
By the Grace of God
the side of the semi says,
cab and trailer lettered
separately,
each avowing half the truth
this great truth
that beef moves only by the grace of God,
that I smell
behind this rolling cage of cattle
the odor of sanctity
God's own gravy
on the hoof
at speed ahead of me.

Why a Golden Calf?

What of the great
brazen wasp,
the silver sparrow,
jasper puppy
or the fat
lead cat?
What of the copper partridge?
No more smoke
and promises
they said,
No more pelicans
and bread.
Enough of that.
Come down off the mountain
or we'll make
another pharaoh.

Robo Dog

I have a mechanical spaniel
that I call
down the alleys of the moon
and savannas black and bright.
I track him over dusty seas.
He comes to me sometimes red,
rolling his eyes like coins
in his sockets.
I save him
from himself
at every turn
and pet his pressed metal head.
He skitters to me
down a deep ravine
to gobble bolts and brackets
from my hat
as only a mechanical spaniel can.

Out of Sight, Out of Mind

The new library's entrance is to be free of books.
Chancellor's orders.
The new facility will be new through and through, new glass, new
people to see through the glass, new listening and viewing rooms
and conduit, new traffic patterns, fees and fines, crash bars,
alarms and security, new security, new membership in good
standing in every access (the hottest engines), no eating,
drinking, anything in the carrels, in every way the way new
newness looks.
Except for the floors that are wasted on books.
We track them to eliminate whatever doesn't circulate, but they're
tenacious and they stink.
They stink like wood.
Like autumn's useless leaves.
They stink as if they'd fill the building with their smell, and if we
didn't filter it they would.
Someday we'll abate them like asbestos, like the uneaten sandwiches
they are.

A week is all we'd need and our students need the work, uneaten sandwiches they are.

Think of it, floor on floor in unimpeded light.

Think of it, the beauty of the new in free fall through the future in its final flight.

For Their Lives

Through the drizzle and the fog all day the peasants fled the front.
Top-heavy carts on the cobbles, oxen, men
under bundles, packs, birds
in their cages.
Wet cats on the bundles, dogs, wobbly goats, a goose, another,
children in their trances as the weather set and the white moon
rose on the vineyards.
Down the center of the dark, doomed,
abandoned town they trundled
under my window.
Midnight I went out to find a gathering of lamps and hammers after
something shook the building: faces in the yellow light around a
leaning overloaded wagon with a broken axle.
Trunks under tight-sewn sacks of grain, rolled rugs, a keg, a chair,
a copper basin, skillets, jugs, a bugle, a bucket of rusty chain,
and roped on top a cage in which a fitch ran round and round.

Poison

When I was little
I saw poison
in a movie and thought
it was a substance.
Where did it come from
I thought
and where could I get some?
Later I learned
it is not a substance
but something
people
do.

Sacred Music Genius

A sacred music genius shot himself today
after a standoff with police.
—National Public Radio News, 17 December 2004

Not just any genius.
A sacred genius of music.
He'd been asking for it for years, to hear the unhearable.
His genius lay in waiting (for the still small voice, sacred bird,
secret tweet).
Light would sing and its agony would be sweet.
But it sounded like cement.
He sank, swam, sank again in air hard as carbide.
He didn't have a prayer.

Church of San Solitudo

I am an abbot.
My cassock is ceramic and my finger bears a golden molar.
Visitors kiss it.
Visitors are unwelcome in my walls.
When my limestone sighs for me, my demons
wake and shape themselves
and I fasten them over my portal.
Their grinning ribs are stiff, as are their frozen lips (as worms are
frozen by the sun).
The vault above the altar lifts me, melted, and paints my pillars with
deadly sins.
My capitals are bitten with my own corrosion.
My body watches me.
Thus I serve my murdered shepherd, crooking the heads of hell and
sucking their brittle blood.
They are so hot my hands are glass.
My lungs are caked with the wind they break.
When my body dies at last and shatters on
the flags, and my ember bud
ascends, I will leave the legions steaming in the stone.
You are neither mortal nor alone.
You are unwelcome in my walls.

The Problem with the Hippo

*The hippo appeared regularly at two or three
minute intervals, always in the same place,
breathed, and immediately sank. This con-
tinued for an hour. We could not make out
what he was doing.*
—T. Roosevelt

The problem with the hippo
is that when you shoot it
it sinks.
Sometimes it never resurfaces
resting in the muck
and waiting
on whatever did for it
or it belly-ups and floats and the porters row it ashore.
Or it moves the lagoon
in a wide green wake,
teeth like pegs in a hungry rush
of pink.
Yesterday was dispiriting,
Angoni gored
by a rhino cow.

This morning though
we found fresh trenches
over thorns and through
the tendrils.
It meant us mischief
and I took it coming on,
water boiling forward off its whiskers.
This afternoon
Nakuru found it floating
in a cove.
I found a pygmy dormouse
in my Iliad—
graphiurus parvus
who'd had his way with the pigskin
binding—and mounted him here
in my tent
by my elephant shrew.

Somewhere Here

On the third day the
conquerer moved his bowels
in his metal hat. He thought
perhaps he'd swallowed his crucifix
and wanted to catch it.
Somewhere here
he knew there was another
province of pain
and prayed for it like
bark for a tree.
By night the sky was off the map
and by day it lay like a belly on the trees.
North was in the earth
where he laid the men the river didn't eat.
The deep's weeks of weather
had been long enough to teach
a taste for leather. All along
the body of the Lord
lay waiting here
heavy with iguanas,
jaguars, hungry vines and
bite-sized gold
he hoped
in unguarded heaps.

If not, a tree of it then
with open arms
wet with heavy leaves.
Would it be round a bend in the river?
Would he wake to it
in a moonlit breeze
or spy it
on the far side of a valley?
Would there be more leaves
than he could carry?

Stuck with Him

Gathered round
a flat stone in the sun
or a well
or a table in an inn
we wonder
what he'll say
this time.
"Fisherman!" Judas shouts
or shakes his head and mutters
"netmender"
laughs and slaps
Nathaniel on the head
so hard
he coughs up his bread.
"Figsucker."
His eyes are like
something coming,
like dead hands.
He's the only
one who ever says
"Don't write that down."

Last Night at Pliny's

Pastry heads of senators packed with raisins.
Pies of beating turtle hearts.
Rubies and saffron in thrushes' eggs.
Flamingos' tongues.
I stuffed a dozen wombs with quinces and
mallows and floated them in a
wine-filled swine in the fountain.
My master's fountain flowed with red Falernian and blood.
He lapped it laughing with his dogs.
The dancers laughed, and the acrobats, and the jugglers juggled
cutlets to the cats.

Swinburne Remembers Digging up Rosetti's Wife

Here is where we buried her
and brought her up again.
Opened her to see her
more for what she was
than what she was.
Dante got right in with her.
We were dirty to our bones,
slow learners
old enough to know
the dead are best left
alone—
as they are—
even if
(especially if) the dead
are friends.

Gadarene Gardener

The demons weren't a problem for my father, nor for his father before
him.
The Jews kept their distance too, which is why our cemeteries were so
lively.
Legions whispered in the tombs but minded their own business in the
bodies.
I minded my business too, pruning figs, tying vines, reciting
necessary formulas to keep the pigs away.
I did it for the pigs, poor pigs who knew no better than to root
around the tombs.
They died the day the Hebrews came.
They bunched up in a herd with worried eyes and waited for their
orders, foaming at the mouth.
They were worthless now—nobody'd eat
them—and as they dove into the
bay I wished again the Romans would close our borders.

Mayan Time (AD 900)

Dawns and dawns I walk
the high white road
to Uxmal.
Clods of jade
and blades of black glass
buy balls of smoke.
I cut myself
again
and again
and sometimes
the winged one
tells me when
I am.
Nothing starts or follows
on a wheel
in a wheel
under a wheeling sky,
no line gone out
but Yum Kaax and Bahlam,
Kukulkan and Huracan
and the Four Hundred Boys
in the Pleiades
drunk again.

The Dungseller and the Scarab

From a lump of dung
a beetle nips
its bit of dough
and rolls it away.
This is all the sun god wants.
The blinding eye is not a greedy god.
Piece here
piece there
enough to light a lamp
in a waterclock,
sacrifice sufficient
for a lucky day.
Or if need be
on a thong round
my neck
I've a bug eternal
in a cedar pod.

Vincent, Confined, Writes that Everything Is Fine

Excepting the wind,
yellow as a bat is black
and shrill
as a tulip.
Especially in my sleep.
I dream of wooden shoes
on a blood-green sea.
Olive into pink and fleshy chrome
O to paint a shining shovel!
The mayor came
with a petition yesterday
to keep me
where I am
as if back with my canvas
I'm a dangerous man.

Alert

Soon I'll have no neighbors
Hitler thinks
pissing in the snow
by his armored car
and smiling.
At last Poland is no neighbor.
Neither are the Czechs a dagger in the back.
That's what a neighbor is.
What everybody is.
These trees are closing in.
Why I wasn't warned
about them
I'll find out this afternoon.
I'll know the names of all the trees.

Johnny Appleseed

Balls of praise to the Lord.
Fruit of knowledge
food of doom.
Balls of praise.
They raise themselves
and when they fall
from grace
red and green
they are exactly what they seem,
old as earth
sweet as the sins
of our fathers.
God's balls.
Gather, save their
seeds and bury
them
and up they come.

Whenever It's Like This

The wind was just like this
the day the tractor flipped.
The mud was just like this.
I disremember
why I thought
we needed such an early start
as if to get ahead
we had to get away with something.
We could have waited out
the rainy spring
the way our neighbors did.
He'd be fifty now and mad
about the price of beans,
both of us
about the price of beans.
I hooked the chain the way
I'd always
told him never to,
so sure
we were to get away with it.

We'd Never Hear the End of It

Close the switch, Czito, now!
—Nikola Tesla, 1899

The apparatus gulped and our hair stood on end.
My scalp was a cap of maggots.
Nikola's eyes were white.
The secondary went bright
red, then a sulphur smell
and a dull blue light
as the mast ignited and
our shoes got hot.
Lightning in my head
was like a kind of metal.
To this day I taste it.
To this day
if only we'd have bled
the dynamo
before it fused itself!
What another nature you'd have seen!

Time Was

Only lately I'm in history
here at the end
so far.
I've looked into it: before my birthdate
nothing, as if I missed the Great Vowel Shift.
The Tulip Craze, the Poor Laws
Middle Passage and Vandals
came and went.
The steam hammer and the chastity belt
and surgery by barbers
the Great Compromise and all of Gondwanaland.
I missed the Wars of the Roses
pyramids and Schisms
never met a wet nurse or the Father of Radio.
I suffered no Great Depression.
I've no memory of the Rape of Nanking
the Teapot Dome or the Lord Protector.
Only lately I wait it out
out of the way (if I can)
of wreckage's momentum
day after day
time
and time again.

When We Find Life Elsewhere

It will be mercurial.
Unexpected.
Life unlike life.
Myths will grow
like lichen on our lander's clock
and every second will surprise us.
A filament of worry
will weigh
more than a walking rock.
Laughter will snow.
We will drill
clean through and out
the other side
to stars again
and will argue over what
we didn't see.

In Case of Lions

The sign says
in case of an encounter do not
(1) panic
(2) run
(3) make eye contact, but
(4) speak in a low, firm voice and
(5) make yourself look large.
If this doesn't work
I try to look
like a rocket.
I once looked like a rabbi
in the moonlight
for almost twenty minutes
with a warm wet muzzle
in my groin.
I've been an ashtray
a prayer card
a nickel
and a bar of soap
anything but me.
Once I hid in my pocket.

Don't Get Smart with Me

The raven rips
his hotdog in half
and hops
to the birdbath
to dip it, watches
the drips ripple, drops
it and looks at me,
a hat with a head
in it
halfway to the garden
and, he knows, his T-bone
bone under the bee tree.
Don't get smart with me
the raven says
You're no different
you eat the dead.

Freeworry

What if now
the house falls down,
four a.m., carpenter ants
in the rafters
as I sit here
fearing? Tomorrow
I could lose
my mind, misplace it
like a satchel
in a strange land
and plough into a crowd.
I need to stay
prepared in case of
massed attack
and think of everything
that hasn't happened
yet.

The Best Years of Your Life They Said

So what
if you don't know what
you've got
till it's gone?
What's wrong with that?
Why know loss
unless lost?
Feeling lucky is
itself
lucky
like it or not.
Take it for granted.
Luck's for the
undeserving
after all
and has
been all along.

Fez

A wad of
cellophane
on a gust along the
gutter
passes
glittering
in the dust.

After it
a small boy
bald
as an old man
laughs
as he catches
and licks it.

The Age of Steam

When I was small enough to sit
in the sink or put both my feet
into a shoe, my father made me
an engine that fit
in a matchbox,
cast and milled
and polished every part.
It looked like an artificial cricket.
To this day
when it idles in my hand
it hops
like a fluttering heart.

Learning Long Division

Seven apples cannot feed a dozen horses
nor equally malnourish them.
Two men cannot share a woman
even on paper.
I can only cross one threshold at a time.
A murder of crows on a carcass
is a black bouquet
cleaning bone. A sunburnt
liver jerked
to slivers feeds them all at once
and each alone,
a good October body
to divide without sharing, tough
but fatty, just enough.

Everything All at Once

If a siskin laid a nuthatch egg
wars would cease,
thoughts would be simpler
almost meaningless,
turtle chicks
chanting
in their hives,
beans bleeding,
apples screaming in the cider press.
If a siskin laid a nuthatch egg
dwarves would run
from stumps
and living things be new
and unpredictable again
for once,
deeply nuts
unknown again as when
men were as trees, walking
and plants were still at peace.

Autumn

It is harder if you try
to keep the leaves.
Let them go.
I've tried to eat them
packed them in freezer bags
filled my mattress
filled my pants
done what I could to revive them
root them
reattach them
wet them again
and green them up.
I must be doing something wrong.

Near the End

He thought he was living
on a boat
floating in the corn.
From the car he walked
a kind of
gangway to the porch.
To my father
this meant
he was afloat
in the ocean.
He was wrong
about the boat.
Right about the ocean.

Making It

An ancient undead
elm holds a honeybee
swarm.
Years ago when
the Red Death struck
they quarantined their tree
posted guards
and kept their own counsel.

Deep in their hollow they
waited it out
put their experts to
work in the brood combs
breeding immunity.

Queens competed round the clock.

Late at night even
in midwinter if I pressed my
ear to the bark
I could hear them focusing
their sugar.

Now they froth
on the stub of a lost
limb where their
entrance is
where they vent
the air they fan
up through their tree
to help it
concentrate.

Low Down on the Sistine Wall

In the lower
left the rising dead
lift their heads
dirt in their hair
half the flesh back
on their bony jaws.
Some look only
weary, unbelieving, nerves
long gone
and skin like vellum
on their bones.
This one lifts
the lid of his crypt
on his back.
Some sit stunned
and stare
with their sockets
waiting on their eyes.
Early risers are
already winding in the sky
like air alive
and kicking.

Staying Out of It

Were I a character
in a story
I'd never appear.
Were I mentioned
I'd always be somewhere
else.
Remember Ahab
on the other side
of the ceiling?
Then he called a meeting
and we saw
he was only
Gregory Peck.
Remember when Oedipus
was just a gloomy rumor,
a stranger,
bad luck
at a distance?
Had he only kept his distance.

Haiku

People want to pro
tect and preserve our many
footprints on the moon.

Birdwatching—sometimes
it gets on my nerves, the way
they perch there, watching.

Unicycle guys
always look alike, like guys
on unicycles.

To save my favor
ite thing I had to change it.
I could not save it.

Glass is viscous. It
sags. Flows. In a million years
our windows will have

puddled and in a
hundred million years they will
all be sand again.

If over time the
sun gave us eyes, the earth must
have given us feet.

Robin pausing on
an elastic worm wonders
what I'm looking at.

Calvin Coolidge had
a raccoon to whom he con
fided who knows what.

Long ago no groups
existed. Nothing looked like
anything at all.

We saw Pluto then,
cold as bones of airless ice,
and continued on.

Having bitten all the
beer in the cooler the bear
thinks he owns the place.

I don't know if we
made it where we were going
but we made it back.

This cricket sounds like
a garbage truck backing up
to a dumpster.

Joy is everything
no matter what. Sadness nothing
no matter what.

Only afterwards
you'll know it was the moment
you were living for.

After the crowd ate
the miracle-fish, what did
they do with the bones?

Does this bug which
hardly moves embody patience
or forgetfulness?

Beetle grubs in their
slow progress just below the
bark live in their bread.

Stepping in a stag
nant spring in breezeless heat I
smell a kind of pus.

This morning was just
this morning and I forget
what I did with it.

A tuft of clover
blows a hole in the pavement,
venting a blossom.

Too soon I've put it
off this long. Is it already
too late at last?

I can't stop in the
traffic for the little book
open in the road.

Thanks to gravity
rock tides rise and fall on the
moons of Jupiter.

Scorpion eats the
deadened cricket, turning it
like an ear of corn.

Deflated Santa
flat on his face in the yard.
Stand back. Give him air.

Printed in the United States
by Baker & Taylor Publisher Services